SHOW OF STRENGTH
THEATRE COMPANY

presents

SO LONG LIFE

by Peter Nichols

First performed at The Tobacco Factory,
Bedminster, Bristol
Wednesday 20 September 2000

Show Of Strength Theatre Company Ltd, 74 Chessel Street,
Bedminster, BRISTOL BS3 3DN. Tel: 0117 902 0235
Registered Charity No 1067886
Registered Company No. 2889027

southwest arts

SO LONG LIFE

by Peter Nichols

CAST IN ORDER OF APPEARANCE

Alice	Stephanie Cole
Greg	Christian Rodska
Jill	Elaine Donnelly
Wendy	Christina Greatrex
Imogen	Lisa Coleman
Mark	Ian Curtis

The play is set in Clifton, Bristol in 1995.
There will be one interval of 20 minutes.

Director	Jenny Eastop
Designer	James Helps
Casting Director	Irene East

Show of Strength would like to thank the following for their help in developing
SO LONG LIFE in December 1999: Wendy Brierley, Constance Chapman, Manon
Eames, Edwina Ford, Penny Gold, Claire Marchionne, Alan Moore, Matthew Thomas.

A radio version of SO LONG LIFE was broadcast on Radio 4 on 28 April 2000.

Peter Nichols

Peter Nichols was born in Bristol in 1927 and educated at Bristol Grammar School, Bristol Old Vic Theatre School and Trent Park Teacher Training College, Herts.

His first television play, WALK ON THE GRASS, was produced in 1959 by the BBC. Many others followed, including PROMENADE, BEN SPRAY, THE HOODED TERROR, THE GORGE, HEARTS AND FLOWERS and THE COMMON.

His first play for the stage, produced in 1967, was A DAY IN THE DEATH OF JOE EGG, which was roughly based on the half-life of his firstborn, Abigail, who lived only until she was 11. Later came THE NATIONAL HEALTH (RNT), FORGET-ME-NOT-LANE (Apollo and Greenwich), CHEZ NOUS (Globe), THE FREEWAY (RNT), HARDING'S LUCK (from E Nesbit; Greenwich), PRIVATES ON PARADE (RSC), BORN IN THE GARDENS (Bristol Old Vic and the Globe), POPPY (RSC), A PIECE OF MY MIND (Apollo) and BLUE MURDER (Show Of Strength).

CATCH US IF YOU CAN was his first film screenplay, followed by GEORGY GIRL (co-author with Margaret Forster, 1966), JOE EGG, THE NATIONAL HEALTH and PRIVATES ON PARADE.

He is the recipient of the John Whiting Award 1967, the Evening Standard Best Play Award 1967, 69, 78 and 82, Society of West End Theatre Awards 1978 and 82, and Ivor Novello Award for Best Musical for POPPY (1985). A DAY IN THE DEATH OF JOE EGG won two Tony Awards when it was revived on Broadway in 1985. He has directed revivals and premieres of six of his plays.

He is a Fellow of the Royal Society of Literature. A memoir, FEELING YOU'RE BEHIND, was published in 1984. He is currently working on a musical based on the songs of Hoagy Carmichael, and The Gulbenkian Foundation has invited him to write a play about genetic engineering. In spring 2000 PASSION PLAY, originally produced by the RSC in 1981, had a triumphant revival at The Donmar and in the West End. His forty or so diaries are in the theatre archives of the British Library, and a selection is published by Nick Hern Books (October 2000).

Stephanie Cole

Stephanie Cole was brought up in the West County and trained at Bristol Old Vic Theatre School. She has a formidable list of theatre credits which include ROSE starring Glenda Jackson (Duke of Yorks); NOISES OFF (Savoy Theatre); STEEL MAGNOLIAS (Lyric Theatre); THE RELAPSE (Old Vic). In 1995 she starred as 'Betty' in A PASSIONATE WOMAN by Kay Mellor which, following brilliant notices, played to packed houses at the Comedy Theatre throughout an extended nine month run. In 1996 Stephanie created the role of 'Angela Parsons' in the world premiere of Peter Schaffer's play WHOM DO I HAVE THE HONOUR OF ADDRESSING? at the Chichester Festival Theatre.

Stephanie's television work has been equally diverse although she is probably best known for her roles in the hugely popular series TENKO and WAITING FOR GOD - for which she won the British Comedy Award for Best Actress. She also played the redoubtable 'Mrs Featherstone' opposite Ronnie Barker's 'Arkwright' in BBC's OPEN ALL HOURS, the tipsy 'Betty Sillitoe' in Yorkshire TV's A BIT OF A DO, and received great personal acclaim for her portrayal of 'Muriel' in Alan Bennett's monologue SOLDIERING ON. Her other TV roles include MEMENTO MORI, THE RETURN OF THE ANTELOPE, IN THE COLD LIGHT OF DAY, GOING GENTLY and POIROT.

In 1999 Stephanie toured with Stephanie Beacham in EQUALLY DIVIDED by Ronald Harwood, and more recently she co-starred with Sir Donald Sinden, Angela Thorne and Alec McCowen in Ronald Harwood's play QUARTET which had a successful run at the Albery Theatre.

Stephanie starred as 'Peggy' in the two series of KEEPING MUM for BBC1, and next year will co-star with Richard Wilson in a new series for BBC1 entitled OTHER ANIMALS written by Michael Aitkins who also wrote WAITING FOR GOD. Her autobiography A PASSIONATE LIFE came out in 1998.

Lisa Coleman *(Imogen)*

Lisa lives in Bristol and trained at the Anna Scher Theatre School.

Television: Series regular as Jude in CASUALTY and Sarah in UNDERCOVER HEART. Other credits include FRENCH AND SAUNDERS; ABSOLUTELY FABULOUS; SEVEN DEADLY SINS and REDEMPTION (all for the BBC); PEAK PRACTICE (Carlton); LONDON'S BURNING (LWT); TRAVELLERS BY NIGHT (TVS) and THE CHIEF (Anglia TV).

Radio: NO COMMITMENT (five series for Radio 3); DOUBLE ACT; ORCHESTRA PALOMA; THE OLD DOG AND PARTRIDGE; FEMALE COMPANY and DOG EAT DOG (all Radio 4); KEEP ON RUNNING and GRIEF (Radio 5)

Film: JOINT VENTURE (Twerly Productions)

Ian Curtis *(Mark)*

Trained: Drama Centre, London

Theatre: TATTOOED EARS (Royal Court Theatre), RAGE (Bush Theatre)

Television: Series regular as Ray Sykes in two series of HOLBY CITY (BBC), and as Corporal Hobbs in SOLDIER SOLDIER (Carlton). Other credits include PIE IN THE SKY (SelecTV), A TOUCH OF FROST and FRONTIERS (Carlton TV), THE GOVERNOR (Yorkshire TV), MEDICS and CRACKER (both for Granada).

Film: Lead role in BRAVO TWO ZERO (Distant Horizon/BBC)

Elaine Donnelly *(Jill)*

Elaine was born and brought up in Gloucestershire, and made her first professional appearance at the Everyman in Cheltenham whilst still at school. She has since worked in plays from Shakespeare to Sam Sheppard, Restoration Comedy to Ayckbourn, in theatres throughout the country. Her most recent work includes TEETH LIKE RAZORS (a celebration of the works of Brecht and Weill) and a tour of WOMEN ON THE VERGE OF HRT. Her television work encompasses three educational series for the BBC, situation comedies, single films and, more recently, NO BANANAS and the highly acclaimed series BETWEEN THE LINES - both for the BBC. Elaine also has a lively voice-over career, and hugely enjoys coaching children for film and television.

Jenny Eastop *(Director)*

Jenny Eastop graduated from Manchester University in 1985 with two main interests, new writing and Renaissance theatre.

After several years working in stage management, she moved into directing new writing for companies such as Hull truck, West Yorkshire Playhouse, Paines Plough, Show Of Strength and the London New Play Festival.

Following work on Renaissance plays at the RSC and National Theatre as Assistant Director to Jude Kelly, Matthew Warchus and Roger Michell, Jenny directed two Middleton comedies at the National Theatre Studio and now regularly directs staged readings for Shakespeare's Globe and Globe Education Department.

Other recent work includes directing Moliere's DON JUAN at the Gatehouse, London, in a new translation by Maya Slater.

Christina Greatrex *(Wendy)*

Theatre: RSC, West End & rep includes Lady M, MACBETH, Cheltenham; Hedda, HEDDA GABLER, Derby; Ruth, THE NORMAN CONQUESTS, Guildford; Gwendolyn, THE IMPORTANCE OF BEING EARNEST, Nottingham; Lady Audley, LADY AUDLEY'S SECRET, Actors Company; Maggie, OCTOBER SONG and Mrs Loveit, THE MAN OF MODE, both for The Orange Tree; Maxine, STEPPING OUT, The Mill at Sonning; Lettice, LETTICE AND LOVAGE, DEATH & THE MAIDEN, BED AMONG THE LENTILS, Mrs Alving, GHOSTS -all Northampton; Madame Arcardina, THE SEAGULL, Greenwich; Ros, PEOPLE ON THE RIVER, The Finborough; Madame X, THE STRONGER, The Latchmere.

TV includes: CORONATION STREET; BOON; WITHIN THESE WALLS; TAKE THREE GIRLS; EMMERDALE; HOWARD'S WAY; HUNTER'S WALK; BBC PLAYS FOR TODAY; RUMPOLE; HOUSE OF ELLIOT

Film includes: IF TOMORROW COMES; BULLSHOT; BETTER DAYS (HTV)

James Helps *(Designer)*

Trained at Wimbledon School of Art 1971-1974. On graduating took up an Arts Council Bursary at Stratford East and the Connaught Theatre, Worthing. Besides seasons as Head of Design at The Nuffield Theatre, Southampton and The Arts Theatre, Ipswich he has designed over 160 productions as a freelance.

Designer of the Year in Northern Ireland (1989) for THE PLOUGH AND THE STARS and AFTER THE FALL. Previous work for Show of Strength includes STARS IN THE MORNING SKY, TALES OF THE UNDEAD, LET'S DO IT, MEASURE FOR MEASURE, LIVING QUARTERS and MYSTERY OF THE ROSE BOUQUET. Other work at The Tobacco Factory includes A MIDSUMMER NIGHT'S DREAM and KING LEAR.

Film work includes LEON THE PIG FARMER and BEYOND BEDLAM. As co-writer/producer for Fat Chance Productions: MONUMENT (Western lights/HTV).

Other recent work includes coproducing and designing ANATOMY OF A MADMAN at Bristol Old Vic and coproducing MASTERCLASS starring Jane Lapotaire at Bath Theatre Royal.

James recently trained as a teacher and is working at Brislington School.

Christian Rodska *(Greg)*

Christian began his career in 1965 as an ASM at Salisbury rep where Stephanie Cole was a member of the company. Since then he has played in theatres all over the country, and in the West End. Television includes a wide variety of roles from a punk rocker in a musical comedy to Neil Kinnock, and programmes such as WYCLIFFE, SHARPE, TAGGART, TENKO, FOLLYFOOT, THE STARS LOOK DOWN, CASUALTY, BROOKSIDE and THE ROUND TOWER. He has recorded several hundred productions of radio plays, poetry readings, novels for audio cassettes and commentaries for Wildlife programmes. For Radio 4 he recorded a documentary about some friends in St Petersburg who are Russian stuntmen. He lives in Bath, and recent productions for Bristol Old Vic include Leroy in THE LAST YANKEE, Dr Stockman in AN ENEMY OF THE PEOPLE, Boolie in DRIVING MISS DAISY, and all seven male characters in Jim Cartwright's TWO.

SHOW OF STRENGTH AND SO LONG LIFE

66 In 1993 I heard that Peter Nichols apparently had several unproduced plays. I already knew he was a brilliant playwright, that much of his work was set in and around his native Bristol, and I'd read his autobiography FEELING YOU'RE BEHIND. For the better part of three years I stalked his agent, trying to get my hands on those plays. In 1995 I finally got to read BLUE MURDER and would have been prepared to kill to do it. Peter came to Bristol to meet the company's directors, we showed him our then venue, and we had lunch on The Glass Boat. The deal was done with not a drop of blood spilt, and BLUE MURDER opened at Quakers Friars on 1 November 1995. It was a huge success and later had a national tour.

Last year I had this feeling there might be something else, so I wrote to Peter and asked. He sent SO LONG LIFE and that old, murderous instinct resurfaced. We discussed the play at length and decided that in the process of developing it we would get a group of actors together to read it privately. SO LONG LIFE's central character is 85 year old Alice - a huge and very demanding role. I sent a script to Connie Chapman who lives in Bristol and has appeared in a number of productions of Peter's work. She rang to say she loved the play but couldn't do it as she'd just come out of hospital after an operation on her knee and couldn't walk. That seemed a trivial excuse, so I suggested we come to her and I'd provide the chairs if necessary. A couple of weeks before Christmas, twelve of us assembled at Connie's flat and spent the day reading and talking about the play. In the course of working on the script Peter also produced a radio version of SO LONG LIFE. This was recorded in Clifton, Bristol and broadcast on Radio 4 in April with Connie Chapman as Alice.

Meanwhile, Show of Strength was gearing up to produce the stage play in the autumn. When Peter suggested Stephanie Cole I never imagined for a moment that she would be available, prepared to work for the Show of Strength stipend, or that she would roll up her sleeves and embrace an old tobacco factory in Bedminster with such enthusiasm. But I took a deep breath and sent the script - and back came the response that this was a wonderful play and she'd love to do it. I've wanted Jenny Eastop to direct a production for Show of Strength for several years, and it's great to have James Helps back designing for the company.

It's been a fascinating year seeing SO LONG LIFE in various stages and versions and getting it this far. I'd like to thank everyone involved in the play's development and production for their time, talent, tolerance and commitment, particularly Peter Nichols, Connie Chapman and Stephanie Cole, who have been a joy to work with. As Oscar Wilde, Lewis Carroll - or perhaps even Peter Nichols - might have said, 'To find one perfect Alice is fortunate, to find two, sublime.' 99

Sheila Hannon, August 2000

SHOW OF STRENGTH
THEATRE COMPANY

THEATRE THAT'S CLOSE ENOUGH TO TOUCH

SHOW OF STRENGTH THEATRE COMPANY was founded in Bristol in 1986 and in 1989 opened a pub theatre at the Hen & Chicken in Bedminster. The company moved to Quakers Friars in the city centre in 1995 and, in 1998, created the theatre at The Tobacco Factory - just a few hundred yards from our first permanent home. The focus has always been on new and rarely performed work. There have now been eleven seasons of productions and readings of work in development. Production highlights include:

- STARS IN THE MORNING SKY, new Russian play later produced by the RSC
- INKLE AND YARICO, a 'lost' eighteenth century anti-slavery musical
- Brock Norman Brock's HERE IS MONSTER, directed by Mark Ravenhill
- English premieres of work by Irish writers Brian Friel, Frank Dunne and Bernard Farrell
- UK Premieres of new Australian plays by Louis Nowra, Michael Gow & Nick Enright UK premiere of Maxwell Anderson's KEY LARGO
- First revival of Githa Sowerby's A MAN AND SOME WOMEN (1914)
- World premiere Fanny Burney's A BUSY DAY (1801) - later Bristol Old Vic/West End
- World premiere Peter Nichols's BLUE MURDER -later national tour
- UK premiere THE SUBSTANCE OF FIRE by Jon Robin Baitz-coproduction with Theatre Royal, Plymouth
- World premiere SAME HOLE DEEPER by Graham Alborough -later Nuffield, Southampton
- BLAVATSKY'S TOWER by Moira Buffini -later commissioned by RNT & RSC
- THE PRICE OF MEAT by Michele Celeste -later Riverside Studios

AWARDS

1990   £5000 ABSA/BSIS Award for attracting a major new arts sponsor

1993   £16,000 London Weekend Television Award for the world premiere of Fanny Burney's A BUSY DAY (1801)

1994   Building A Better Bristol Award for bringing theatre to a culturally deprived area of the inner city

1995   Building A Better Bristol Award (jointly with Bristol City Council) for successfully establishing a new theatre venue in Bristol

1997   £7500 Guinness/Royal National Theatre Award for Pub Theatre for the European premiere of Nick Enright's GOOD WORKS

1998   VENUE magazine's Best Production from the Region for THE LAST APACHE REUNION

1999   VENUE magazine's Best Production from the Region and The Independent Drama Association's Best Production in Bristol for BLAVATSKY'S TOWER

ELSIE & NORM'S MACBETH

by John Christopher Wood

Classic-Scottish-Tragedy turns Classic-Yorkshire-Comedy

Join Elsie and Norman in their living room for a hilarious reworking of The Scottish Play. More Dunroamin than Dunsinane, Shakespeare a la Grimethorpe comes complete with poetry, singing, dancing and tasteful soft furnishings - plus full supporting cast of endangered species.

First performed more than twenty years ago (Reduced Shakespeare Company eat your hearts out), the play had a national tour starring Gordon Kaye.

John Christopher Wood is a regular contributor to VENUE magazine and is Chair of Bath Fringe. The success of ELSIE & NORM'S MACBETH led to a commission from Liverpool's Everyman Theatre for NO HOLDS BARD, with Drew Schofield and Michael Starke. This is the first Bristol production of a highly praised and funny play.

'It was for plays like this that God created comedy.'
WHAT'S ON BIRMINGHAM

'...a wonderful absurd parody in wincing bad taste... very funny indeed.' -THE SCOTSMAN

Aftershow Talkabout: Wed 1 November   Matinee: Sat 11 November

---

Sat 18 November - Sat 2 December

NICHOLODEON

A celebration of the words and music of Peter Nichols

A rare treat from one of Britain's greatest playwrights: a literary and musical cabaret created by Peter Nichols especially for Show of Strength. As well as the famous works (PRIVATES ON PARADE, THE NATIONAL HEALTH, POPPY, A DAY IN THE DEATH OF JOE EGG, BORN IN THE GARDENS), NICHOLODEON includes previously unproduced and unpublished work - as well as four new songs.

Born in Bristol in 1927, Peter Nichols has written over sixty original plays, musicals and adaptations for stage, cinema, television and radio. Accolades include four Evening Standard Best Play Awards, two Society of West End Theatre Awards, and a Tony Award (Broadway).

NICHOLODEON will be directed by Peter Nichols and performed by local actors and musicians including Andrew Hilton, Kate McNab, Alan Moore, John Telfer and Amy Wadge. Much of the material is set in Bristol and includes extracts from Peter Nichols's autobiography FEELING YOU'RE BEHIND as well as the first volume of his DIARIES, published this October.

Peter Nichols's work combines incisive humour with great theatricality and NICHOLODEON is, above all, a wonderful entertainment celebrating a body of work spanning more than 40 years.

Aftershow Talkabout: Wed 29 November   NB: No Matinee

AGE Concern
Bristol

Canningford House, 38 Victoria Street, Bristol BS1 6BY

Age Concern Bristol provides a range of services:

- Advice and Information   ☎ 0117 922 5353
- Simple garden maintenance   ☎ 0117 929 2552
- Names of vetted tradespeople   ☎ 0117 929 2552
- Befriending   ☎ 0117 929 7537
- Home, Travel, Motor & Life Insurance   ☎ 0117 922 1933
- Day care at the Roundhouse, Stockwood   ☎ 01275 834 668

VOLUNTEERS NEEDED

Have you got some time to spare?

Want to learn new skills?

Want to help older people to make the most of their lives?

Age Concern Bristol is looking for volunteers, of any age, to help with a variety of services provided for older people in Bristol.

We can offer you:

- Support and training
- A friendly, relaxed atmosphere
- An up to date reference if you are job hunting
- Travel expenses and free tea and coffee!

If you are interested in becoming a volunteer, please call us for an informal chat on **0117 929 7537.** We would love to hear from you.

AGE CONCERN INSURANCE
0117 922 1933

We can offer you low cost travel insurance and motor breakdown insurance whether you are 25 or 105!

If you are over 55, we can also offer you low cost insurance for:-

- Buildings
- Contents
- Motor
- Life

Not only do you get a good deal, but your money supports our services for older people in Bristol.

Although part of the Age Concern movement, Age Concern Bristol is a small, independent organisation. We are self-financing and rely on local support. If you would like to make a donation to help fund our services, please call us on 0117 929 7537 or write to us at the above address.

Peter Nichols

SO LONG LIFE

Characters

ALICE, *b. 1910*

GREG, *b. 1940*

JILL, *b. 1955*

WENDY, *b. 1935*

IMOGEN, *b. 1965*

MARK, *b. 1965*

Place: Greg's and Jill's house in Bristol.

Time: 1995. Sunday. Midday.

The oblqiue sign / indicates that the next speech begins.

ACT ONE

Darkness for some time.

A light flashes offstage, a little escaping, approaches, fills a doorway, floods a living room. One other door. Window in fourth wall. ALICE, *85, one arm in a sling, enters, limping. This light is her consciousness. She's helped in by* GREG, *55.*

ALICE. Oh dear!

GREG. Oh dear! Ohdearohdearohdear!

ALICE (*confused*). What?

He clears an armchair of newspaper, folding and tidying.

What a turn-out. Many happy returns.

GREG. What?

ALICE. I was expecting a surprise. A roomful of people giving me a surprise.

GREG. Here. Sit here.

ALICE *makes her painful way to the chair.*

ALICE. Where's my bag? Did I leave it in the car?

GREG (*calling upwards at the door*). Love! You up there?

ALICE. I think I must have left my bag in the car. Go and fetch it, there's a good boy.

Looks about at the emptiness. GREG *goes on tidying.*

So much for eighty-five long years! Dear Lord!

JILL, *40, comes down from upstairs.*

JILL. Hello, you. What have you been up to now?

ALICE. I had a little fall.

JILL. And been lying there all night, I hear.

ALICE. Not where I fell.

GREG. She tried to lean on the wash-basin and missed . . .
    couldn't get to her feet so dragged herself back across the
    hall to her room and half on to the bed. When I arrived, she
    was sound asleep. (*To* ALICE.) That right?

ALICE. Who's 'she', the cat's mother? I was always taught it
    wasn't nice to say 'she' to anyone's face.

    GREG *shakes head and goes.*

JILL. It's not nice to make us worry about you. You ever heard
    of hypothermia?

ALICE. Where d'you think I live? In the Ark? It's like
    anorexia. All the rage. Like – what's it called? – it starts
    with an 'a' as well –

JILL. Amnesia?

ALICE. Oh, my memory – um –

JILL. Alzheimer's?

ALICE. That's him.

JILL. You could have died!

ALICE. Isn't that what you all want?

JILL. Yes, of course. A.s.a.p. That's why we're so concerned
    about you.

ALICE. Oh, Christine dear . . . I've lived too long.

    JILL *impatiently moves to retrieve the paper* GREG *threw
    out.*

    D'you hear what I said?

JILL. Oh, were you talking to me?

ALICE. Is anyone else here?

JILL. Not to someone called Christine?

ALICE. What?

JILL. Christine was your son's *first* wife. As I think you know very well.

ALICE. Oh dear, I forget. There's your anorexia. Jill, isn't it? It's like I say, I've lived too long.

She dabs away tears with a tissue. JILL *watches.*

JILL. So why don't you take a bus to the Suspension Bridge and end it all? Thousands do.

ALICE. You could die waiting for a bus round here.

She crumples the tissue and looks about. JILL *provides a bin.*

JILL. You could surely afford a taxi. Not as though you'd be saving it for a rainy day, is it? If you were going to end it all?

GREG *comes back with handbag, in which* ALICE *at once rummages, produces cigarettes and lights one.* JILL *provides an ashtray, then mimes opening a window downstage.*

Only you'll have to choose a moment when the guards aren't looking. They've got closed-circuit cameras these days, with so many jumping off.

GREG. What, The Bridge? No prahblem. Wait for a moment when the security men are into a violence video.

JILL. Haven't they raised the railings too? So you'd need a box to stand on. And someone to help you over. The taxi-driver perhaps?

GREG. He'd expect a tip in advance, before you jumped.

JILL. There could be a set fee, like to the airport. One way only, help with climbing the wall, phone-call to relatives – all-in . . . everyone happy.

GREG. Some days I feel I'd like to hold your hand and we could go together. When I next feel that, I'll give you a ring.

JILL (*to* ALICE). His psychotherapist saw through that one straight off . . . asked him when it opened and he hadn't found out, so knew he wasn't serious.

ALICE. It never closes, does it? My grandfather was in the parade the day it opened. Carried his trade across.

JILL and GREG embrace and caress out of ALICE's view.

Oh dear . . . I was expecting such a surprise.

JILL. They're on the way.

GREG. D'you want a drink? No need to wait.

JILL. Sweet sherry?

ALICE. Nice Bristol Cream, yes. Bless your heart. And give me a nice birthday kiss.

JILL and GREG lean over and ALICE gives them each a bear-hug.

You'll take care of my boy, won't you, Christine? When I'm gone. Well, I know you will. You do now.

JILL separates herself.

I mean Jill.

Music.

The light dims to half, as it does throughout when she dozes. GREG takes the cigarette from her fingers, stubs it out.

GREG. Still that vice-like grip . . .

Her eyes are shut, head lolling.

That bear-hug.

JILL. Same way she clings to life.

Light dims further and almost goes out as they watch.

GREG. I can't bear to see you like this.

Dim light returns on GREG and JILL.

The blue-rinse dandelion head . . . chimpanzee dentures . . . eyes swimming like scallops enlarged by the lenses,

JILL. Don't be unkind, Greg –

GREG. – glazed with cataract, . . . torso thickened from so many Mintoes . . . the breasts I must have sucked God knows how often, crêpie now like pebble-dash . . . dainty high-heeled shoes that mean she imagines herself as she once was, on a high-stool, toying with a gin-and-lime.

JILL. A flapper, was it?

GREG. A soubrette. Petite and dainty.

JILL. With tiny feet. She's always looking at them.

GREG. This pretty woman I proudly escorted to cocktail-bars or the New Palace. Men fell for her until she started talking and betrayed the poverty of her intellectual data-bank.

JILL. Try to forgive her for growing old.

He shakes his head; sniffs above her.

GREG. Eau-de-Cologne, yes, still for her the epitome of chic.

A door buzzer sounds. ALICE *wakes, the lights to full.* JILL *goes to kitchen,* GREG *to front door. Voices off, to which* ALICE *listens attentively.*

ALICE. My little girl at last. I knew she wouldn't let her mother down on such a special day . . .

WENDY, *60, enters, followed by* IMOGEN, *late 20s,* MARK, *30, carrying a smart shopping-bag with food and drink.*

WENDY. Well, who's a clever girl? Many happy returns.

She bends to kiss ALICE *and gets the bear-hug.*

So – what's this I hear? Been at the Bristol Milk again?

ALICE. I expected you to be here to surprise me.

WENDY. We wanted to be, Mum, honestly.

IMOGEN (*kissing* ALICE). It was the train, Grandma.

ALICE. Nana.

IMOGEN. Nana.

GREG *returns.*

ALICE. Who d'you think wants to be Grandma? This brazen young hussy at the hospital said 'how old are you, Alice?'

MARK. Twenty-one, aren't you?

ALICE. 'Twenty-one,' I said and it's 'Mrs.Usher' to you. (*Looks at him closely.*) Who are *you*? My daughter's new young man?

MARK. Not that new.

ALICE. Philip, is it? Andrew?

WENDY. Take no notice.

ALICE. Bruce? Mario?

WENDY. She only does it to annoy.

ALICE. Aziz? No.

WENDY. Christ, Mum, those names are from my Paleozoic Era, the prehistoric past. You met Mark when we were down last Christmas.

JILL brings in a glass of dark sherry but puts it aside when she sees MARK has champagne.

JILL. What happened? She expected you to be here / to surprise her.

WENDY (*kissing her*). Don't ask. I mean, how long were we stuck outside Didcot Parkway? Three days?

IMOGEN. About half an hour, in fact. Jill . . .

She kisses JILL too.

WENDY. Parkway is not a lawn or woodland but a place they park their cars for the day, right? Talk about huddled masses yearning to be free. And do you know the reason, the official alibi?

JILL. Leaves on the line?

GREG. 'Police pursuing a culprit on the track'?

WENDY. Wrong! 'The delay to this service is due to the late running of this train'.

ALICE*'s head nods and stays down as the light begins to dim.*

I mean, we're sorry the food's cold. This is due to its not being hot, right? Sorry the train hasn't left the station due to not having moved.

IMOGEN. I heard 'We're looking at the track ahead'. I mean, you sort of hope they do that as a general thing.

WENDY. Isn't pee-arr the most insulting way to keep people in their place?

GREG. You'd know, of course . . .

WENDY *glares at him and is about to answer.*

Black-out.

After a few seconds, dim light returns, some on ALICE. JILL *and* MARK *are missing.*

WENDY (*to* IMOGEN, *quietly*). Is she off?

IMOGEN *nods.* WENDY *speaks to* GREG.

So – you took her to Casualty?

GREG. She was bruised and catatonic. Her upper arm's black with being lain on. She says she was calling most of the night.

IMOGEN. No-one can hear in those insulated flats. She could have died.

WENDY. Okay. That's it. This can't go on. She's a menace to herself. A disaster waiting to happen.

IMOGEN. Poor Gran.

WENDY. I mean, flooding the downstairs flat when she let the bath overflow was bad enough –

GREG. And cutting her finger half-off with the serrated knife.

WENDY. And fusing the power for the whole block?

IMOGEN. Poor Nana.

WENDY. And the dust and stench and that skin of grease like cling-film over everything . . .

IMOGEN. She can't see. Or smell.

WENDY. So this time she must do as we tell her. I can't come rushing down from town whenever she sets fire to the fucking carpet. And why should you two have to cope?

WENDY takes pills from her bag and swills them down with ALICE's *wine.*

Poor Jill, after doing a full-time job –

GREG. – a 25-hour a day, 8 days a week job –

WENDY. – exactly, then to look after her mother-in-law as well. This must tax even *her* infallible social conscience. And how can I feel but guilty as shit for not being here to do my share?

She breaks off, looking at ALICE.

And can I say now, once we've got her settled in the Twilight, she's not to assume she can come to you every weekend for Sunday dinner. We'll make that clear as of now.

GREG. Sunday dinner? Oh –

IMOGEN. Is this the right occasion though? I mean, on her birthday? After she's been lying on the floor all night. She'll be at her most vulnerable.

WENDY. Mind-reader!

GREG. That's all over, the ritual roast. We finally decided enough was enough and told her *we*'ve never had one since we married, then she tells us she prefers Kentucky Fried anyhow.

WENDY. Chicken they love. Her Michelin five-star rating. No higher praise than 'Just like chicken.'

GREG. I liked 'Is this *best* butter?'

WENDY. What was *worst* butter, right?

IMOGEN. I kind-of wish we *did* have Sunday roast.

JILL (*returning with glasses*). The champagne got warm at Didcot so Mark's popped it in the freezer. And I'm heating the snacks / you brought from Soho.

WENDY. That generation weren't cooks. They were food-destroyers. 'Yet here's a taste!' A trace of flavour. Boil it away.

IMOGEN. At least they cooked. Does anyone nowadays?

GREG. Only watch others do it on TV while they eat a curry from a tinfoil dish.

WENDY. Jill, I've just been saying, the hour has come.

JILL. *You*'ve been saying?

IMOGEN. And I say no. She's bruised and vulnerable.

WENDY. Right. Kick her while she's down. Only way. Otherwise she'll beat us every time.

IMOGEN. Good job I know you love her really.

MARK *returns with champagne bottle.*

WENDY. For you, the world is a loving place. Where did your father and I go wrong? We did our level best to set an example of loathing and acrimony. Your compassionate nature must be a throwback. A recessive gene cropping up like haemophilia after a long sleep through me and Nana.

IMOGEN. Piss off. I don't care for this holy virgin character. I'm really not like that at all, trust me.

This speech surprises everyone. MARK *removes the cork and the sound brings* ALICE*'s head up – and the lights.*

ALICE. Not those German buggers again?

IMOGEN. Don't be frightened, Grandma, it's only a cork.

ALICE. Nana.

She takes out another cigarette. MARK *pours champagne.*

WENDY. Still smoking yourself to death?

ALICE. They wouldn't let you in the infirmary. This Chinese
    hussy got up as a nurse said 'That can kill you'. I said the
    sooner the better.

MARK. Twenty-one's a bit soon to give up, surely?

ALICE. I said 'I'm doing my family a good turn.'

    I said, 'They can't wait for me to pop off – '

GREG. You mean, save time by having you lightly toasted
    before we slide you into the furnace?

    He lights her cigarette.

IMOGEN. Oh, Nana, don't listen!

ALICE. I'd sooner that than *burying*. In some messy grave
    nobody wants to see to. Few plastic blooms in a jampot.
    On our Sunday runs, I always told your father 'don't drive
    past any cemeteries. Or churches. Or castles. Thatched
    cottages. Nothing from before the Ark.'

    Rummages without success. JILL *guesses and hands her a
    box of tissues, which she uses to dab her eyes.* IMOGEN
    hugs her and she recovers.

GREG. So, if you're so mad for modern buildings, why d'you
    always say mine are eyesores?

ALICE. We don't want America, do we?

GREG. I thought you did.

ALICE. That's alright in Chicago. Not in Bristol.

GREG. But nothing old. So what *do* you want? Have you any
    idea?

ALICE. Not sharing some estate with a lot of coloureds.
    I notice you don't.

MARK (*giving her a glass of champagne*). Voilà, madame!

ALICE (*looking at it*). Oh, dear.

GREG (*amused*). Oh dear oh dear / oh dear . . .

WENDY. If you two have finished then – and if everyone's glass is full . . . Happy birthday. And many more.

They all toast her and drink. ALICE *coughs, winces, gives an exaggerated shudder.*

ALICE. Lovely. Like that cider we used to drink when I was a girl.

MARK. This is the widow. Veuve Cl*u*cquot,

WENDY. Cl*i*cquot –

MARK. – one of the best champagnes on the market.

ALICE. Well, it would be. Wendy can afford the best, can't you, my love? That's what I always tell Greg when he carries on at the way you waste your money. I say 'well, she can afford to'.

WENDY *gives* GREG *a long-suffering look. He shrugs.*

I don't know why you always bring sour wine / when you know I'd sooner sweet?

MARK. Because only the best is good enough / for you.

ALICE. Or else she wants to show me up as ignorant?

IMOGEN. No, it isn't, Nana, really.

JILL. Would you sooner have this Bristol Cream?

ALICE. Oh, bless your heart, – Jill isn't it?

WENDY. Is that what you were on yesterday? That made you fall down? My God, really! . . . lying there all night!

ALICE. No. That was only a bad dream.

JILL. You don't get bruised by dreams.

GREG (*giving it thought*). Well . . .

ALICE. That's better. That acid-y stuff would give me heartburn.

She belches.

Oh dear. I knew it would. I beg your pardon. That happens when you're getting on.

MARK. Getting on for twenty-two.

WENDY. Can we put that joke to bed, sweetheart? It wasn't funny fifty years ago.

ALICE belches again.

ALICE. I do beg your pardon.

She shakes her head; then it lolls and the light goes.

When it dimly returns, they're all amused, waving away a bad smell.

WENDY. Jesus!

JILL. That's par for the course. Usually in the car.

ALICE (*waking*). Dropped off.

MARK. Dropped *what*?

WENDY. Mark, did you touch base? Be a honey, let Joanna know we've arrived.

MARK. On Sunday?

WENDY. Come on, they're editing that archbishop's obit / all afternoon.

MARK. She won't thank us. They've got the mobile number if anything needs –

She glares and he submits, dials on his cellnet and mutters into it in a corner.

WENDY. And check the trains back home.

ALICE. Home?

MARK. I already did, at the station.

WENDY. Do it again. There could be culprits on the track.

GREG. Bristol Parkway was once the village of Stoke Gifford. It was on the itinerary for Dad's Sunday runs. Now the parish church tower overlooks a commuter car park and Bristol's a London suburb. Mum, d'you remember Stoke Gifford?

Lights brighten. ALICE *shakes her head.*

Or Chipping Sodbury?

ALICE. Talk about a one-horse town.

WENDY. You always called it that as we drove through the high street.

ALICE. The only street.

GREG. We used to look out for it.

IMOGEN. What?

WENDY. The one horse.

GREG. As of now, population sixty thousand.

WENDY. The new Britain you used to advocate.

GREG. Chipping Sodbury? La Ville Radieuse? Shangri-La? In a pig's arse! A dormitory town. Suburb of a suburb, with suburbs of its own.

WENDY. So it didn't turn out as you imagined? It's what the people wanted . . .

GREG. The complex issues of modernism aren't easily summarised in one of your sound-bites. (*Suddenly bright, an announcer.*) 'Tonight we ask . . . why are the cloud capp'd towers of a few years back now being brought low by men with swinging balls? Were they after all the slums of the future?' . . .

Music. The lights dim and ALICE *nods. The others emerge from darkness and their distorted voices merge.*

Light only on ALICE's *face.*

ALICE. Off they go. Talk talk talk. Those two have talked each other's heads off ever since they could toddle. And, by senior school, it was a sort of Double Dutch to anyone else. I was so proud of them, talking so clever, till they started bringing home their friends and I saw they could *all* do it. Only, if I tried to join in, they'd go mute and Wendy'd offer me another cup of tea, like now with the champagne. So I let them get on with it and drift off. Once or twice some

fresh arrival used to toss a remark in my direction, like
I was the cat's mother, but soon as they could they'd turn
back and carry on about books and films and paintings . . .

*She stands and moves down to another light, as though to
escape. Turns to watch* MARK *finish a call, look at the
chattering group and dial again.*

The latest toy boy's like I used to be – longing to join in but
can't get his tongue round the words. But fanciable. I'm not
so old I can't see that. Not much up here but for what he
does that's not where it's needed. Well-hung I'd say. Talk
about swinging balls. Some catch for a woman of sixty.
Dream on, daughter. The sexual charge for him isn't *your*
figure but the ones in your bank account. Except I shan't
say that aloud. I can't wound my little girl, never mind how
easy she hurts me, which is a mother's destiny. Her salary's
in all the papers now . . . a millionairess! – and only for
chattering like she always did.

MARK *finishes the call, looks at* WENDY *and dials again.*

Since Imogen's father cleared off, there's been a dozen boys
like him, half her age and less, all colours of the rainbow,
and all *using* her. In my day fellows had to pass on before
you were free of them. Funny how we outlive them, when
you think of all we go through. They have it easy and die
young. That home they want to put me in is all widows.
A fucking nunnery. There. I can *think* that word, even if
I could never say it aloud the way she says 'periods' and
'abortions' and 'lesbians' on her show for all the world to
hear.

She returns, sits and sleeps. Lights go to black.

*After a few seconds' silence, a burst of laughter wakes her.
Lights come half-on. They've all changed position.*

WENDY. Mark –

MARK. What?

WENDY. D'you get through to Joanna?

MARK. Melissa's still trying the control room.

WENDY. Melissa?

MARK. Joanna's new secretary.

WENDY. I've told you never to mess with menials. That cow's got some fucking sauce, / I must say.

IMOGEN. Don't swear in front of Grandma, Mother.

WENDY. She's asleep surely? She was just now.

IMOGEN. You're not asleep, are you, Nana?

She touches ALICE*'s hair. Lights full as* ALICE *looks at* IMOGEN.

Because guess what, it's Present Time!

ALICE. Oh dear.

GREG. Always 'oh dear'.

ALICE. What?

GREG. When anything's unexpected. Here's your heart's desire. Oh dear . . . everything you've ever longed for . . . oh dear.

JILL. Enough, love . . .

GREG. Magic casements opening on the foam of perilous seas in fairy lands forlorn . . . oh dear oh dear –

ALICE. Where are these presents then?

WENDY. Whoa, not yet. First you have to pay your dues. I have to say a few words. Charge your glasses.

MARK *shares out the rest of the champagne.*

Where shall I begin?

GREG. How about 'Hello, I'm Wendy Usher'?

MARK. We dropped that at the top of the last series.

WENDY. He's winding me up, Mark.

ALICE. Bless his heart! I bet you could bite your tongue off, giving away you haven't watched her programme for a whole year. A kiss for mother.

She makes GREG *embrace her and returns it with a bear-hug.*

WENDY. It's not that I want to, okay? – but I have to explain our gift. So bear with me. I dare say we all know our mother's middle name –

ALICE. Florence.

WENDY. Right, but why?

ALICE. Why *not?* Florence was fashionable then.

WENDY. And there was a very special reason why. I got my team to research your birth year. 1910 is still a mostly horse-drawn world, flying and films both in their infancy, two great wars still ahead . . . Crippen's caught by the new telegraph . . . Churchill sends in the army to put down striking Welsh miners at Tonypandy . . .

ALICE. Best thing, your father always said. Show those idle buggers the big stick.

GREG *and* JILL *are laughing.*

WENDY. Oh, our father, yes, one of the dazzling political intellects of the age. Three hundred and fifty colliers killed in a pit up north and that drunken bastard sends in the troops.

ALICE. Same as dear old Maggie did.

WENDY. No wonder in his early days he admired Hitler.

ALICE. Dad never liked Hitler. How could you?

WENDY. I mean Churchill!

IMOGEN. Come, Mother, all those demagogues admired each *other* – Lloyd George, Bernard Shaw, / H.G. Wells, Mussolini . . .

WENDY. My point exactly: Churchill was essentially despotic. A crypto-Fascist / in a silk hat.

GREG (*incredulous*). A what?

JILL. Leave it, love.

GREG. He was a libertarian adventurer who / prized the parliamentary system . . .

WENDY. You surely won't dispute that he felt only contempt for the people who adored him? It was unrequited love.

JILL. Would there be any point? (*And, as* WENDY *stares.*) Disputing?

GREG (*calmly*). I suppose it is still possible to hold an opinion other than yours?

WENDY (*defensively*). But it's funny yours is *always* the opposite of mine – on principle. No matter what you really think. The moment our views coincide, you do a u-turn. Last time we talked you agreed with me Churchill fought *for* Fascism as long as it wore the red, white and blue.

ALICE. Never mind, my son. (*Kisses and holds his hand, looks at* WENDY.) Be fair to your little brother, Wendy, because he was so wonderful in the war.

JILL. But he can only have been about five when it ended.

IMOGEN. Not Greg. Churchill.

Everyone laughs, which eases the tension. ALICE *sings:*

ALICE. Who is that man with the big cigar?

Da-dum-dee-dum dum de-dum-dum-dum?

I can't remember how it goes on.

WENDY. You never could.

IMOGEN. Mother!

WENDY. Okay. Okay. Bear with me a nanosecond longer. X-rays are in their infancy . . . Edward VII, Mark Twain and Tolstoy die . . . so does the lady with the lamp. And Alice Florence Usher is born.

GREG (*sotto voce*). Some trade-off.

ALICE. Then there was. (*Sings*.)

'Let the people sing
Sing like anything . . .
Da-dee-dum-dee-dum-dum doo . . . '

She shakes her head and drinks. They wait for more.

GREG. Wendy, are you hoping to use Mum in a programme,
remembering the century? Five minutes, tops. Then da-dee-
dum-dee-dum . . .

Lights fade to half as ALICE *tries to remember the words.*

ALICE. Yes, it was:

Any song you darn' well please –
Let the people sing, let the rafters ring,
Da-dee-dum-de-dee –

MARK. That's what Wendy's getting round to. We've
remembered it *for* her. Why d'you think we wanted to lend
those snaps and / old cine-films from Greg?

WENDY (*shutting him up*). Borrow, sweetheart.

ALICE (*sings*).
'What makes a gander meander
In search of a goose?
What makes a lady of eighty
Go out on the loose,
Da-dee-de-dumdy-de-dumby – '

MARK. How about it, Alice?

He shows the videocasette. Lights up to full.

This Is Your Life.

ALICE (*looking for the television*). What, on now? Who is it
this week?

MARK. A film of your fifty golden years.

ALICE. Oh, no. Oh dear . . .

WENDY. This is Mark's baby. Once he heard there were these
old cans in your attic, he went to work like a man
possessed.

MARK. Always makes terrific viewing, okay? People looking at theirselves when young . . . The before-and-after
stills . . . cut from full head of hair to the odd strands /
combed across –

WENDY. Even I haven't seen this assembly.

MARK. The crew's done a great job. Captions and all.

He's been slotting in the cassette then turns down the light.

ALICE (*seeing* JILL *try to leave*). Where's Jill sneaking off to?

JILL. Upstairs. To finish a custody report for case conference,
only I've seen all these videos –

MARK. But not the cans of old film that was in her attic –

JILL. I wasn't even part of the / family then –

WENDY. Come on, Jill. Help you understand the family-from-
hell you married into.

JILL. From hell? You flatter yourselves. Come and meet a
few of my cases . . . babies born with a heroin habit – or
AIDS? . . . trans-sexual fathers . . . demented fourteen-year-
old mothers running berserk with Stanley knives in the
court-house –

ALICE. Oh dear . . .

JILL. – and us solicitors and social workers locked in chambers,
wondering if we'll ever get / to our next hearing . . .

WENDY. They're different. You can be objective about them.
Professional. Like I am about the people on my
programmes.

JILL. But when the closing captions roll, you turn them off,
right? Over and done with. Mine are still there week after
week till we solve the problem. And if we don't and
someone's hurt, you and your sort will demand our heads
on a plate.

WENDY. Cool it, love. I only ever piss on social workers when
there's been / some indisputable miscarriage.

JILL. This one I'm on is a first. A father's defence is that raping his daughter was a valuable part of her sexual education.

IMOGEN (*to* JILL). I can't imagine how you cope. I live such a sheltered life these days.

MARK. Among the dreaming spires?

WENDY. No, that's Oxford, darling. (*Then to* JILL.) I think Mark might be hurt if you walk out when he's worked so hard on what's / meant to be a family present –

JILL. I didn't ask him to. It's not the past we should be bothering with in the few hours we've got together / but what to do about –

ALICE. Wendy, use the brains God gave you. Jill doesn't want to see Greg's first wife coming on and everyone thinking she had three kiddies and Jill's had none and wasn't it selfish of Greg to have that operation?

GREG. Selfish!

IMOGEN. That's crap, Nana. We all know this was a shared decision based on deeply-held convictions –

JILL. Oh, do you? I don't think. No matter how we talk about the extrapolated world population, say by, two thousand-and-ten and the need for global birth-control, it's always 'she treats that cat like the child she never had'.

IMOGEN. You can't honestly believe / that's what we –

JILL. Not you, Imogen. You'd never harbour such an unkind thought.

IMOGEN. Hardly. As at thirty I haven't started a family myself.

GREG. We should never have told her.

JILL. What's the point of making a sacrifice if we don't advertise our reasons?

GREG. The sacrifice was yours, not mine. I already had a boy and two girls.

ALICE. You haven't got them now, though, have you? One married to a Moslem in Indonesia. One in Australia, the other with the starving in Africa. Say what you like, Gregory, children can be a great comfort when you're getting on.

JILL. What the world needs is less people at both ends: at the start less babies and at the end less . . .

She breaks off, looks at ALICE, *standing behind her.*

And I didn't ask you down here for another backward trawl through the Usher family album but to find a practical solution to the custody case no court can solve.

They all look at ALICE. *Light dims to half. Her head lolls.*

IMOGEN. Oh, Jill, we will, I swear. If I have to do it myself.

JILL. What, do your share? Have her to stay? I know you mean well but – honestly – d'you think she'd feel much at home on High Table? Halfway through the Latin grace she'd be wanting a Jimmy.

IMOGEN. I teach at a glorified Poly in Birmingham. Not High Table so much as School Dinners.

JILL. Remember the opening of your first airport terminal, Greg, when the minister was about to unveil the plaque and she asked if anyone knew the whereabouts of the toilet and I didn't dare ignore her even at that wonderful moment in our life together and when I got back it was all over.

GREG. And when they all applauded, she said afterwards 'Oh, yes, they were clapping you, my son, – right in my ear!'. Listen, love, you go and work on your report. There'll still be time after we've watched the film.

JILL. Time? Still time? There's no time!

With an angry cry, JILL *goes, slamming the house door, fully waking* ALICE. *Lights to half.*

ALICE. Those German buggers again?

IMOGEN. Can you see, Nana?

ALICE. Tell you the truth, my eyes – what with glaucoma and cataract, my doctor says – Can we have the lights down?

IMOGEN. They are down.

MARK. Right, look. 1945. The end of World War Two.

WENDY. Dad had just bought the cine-camera.

GREG. No mistaking his distinctive directorial style. Still Box Brownie. Everyone lined up facing the sun. 'Don't anyone move!'

ALICE *shakes her head, laughing.*

WENDY. What's funny?

ALICE. I just thought of that spaghetti harvest. D'you remember, Gregory?

IMOGEN. That what?

GREG. A fight I had with Dad.

WENDY. To the death. You nearly came to blows. An April Fool joke with spaghetti hanging off the trees.

GREG. Being gathered in by peasants. And Dad believed the BBC, rather than his own son who'd lived and worked in Italy.

ALICE. The whole country believed it.

GREG. They only ever saw spaghetti in tins.

WENDY. That was then, this is now. People are smarter. In no small measure thanks / to the media you so enjoy slagging off –

ALICE. Talk, talk, talk –

IMOGEN. Who's this? Nana . . . you, mother . . . and – ?

MARK. Greg, aged ten.

ALICE. Yes, your Uncle Gregory.

WENDY. Uncle? D'you ever think of him as Uncle, Imo?

IMOGEN. So you must be fifteen, Mum.

MARK. You were a beauty, even then, love, that figure, those legs!

WENDY. Oh, this was B.C. Before Cellulite.

GREG. And look at Alice Florence. At what age – forty?

IMOGEN. How pretty you are, Nana! The flowing hair, the slim build.

GREG. I was so proud to escort her.

Light dims. WENDY *sees* ALICE *dozing.*

WENDY. You'd think at least she'd be interested in her *own* life.

IMOGEN. Sssh . . .

GREG. Why?

WENDY. What?

GREG. To be reminded of her youth and the figure she can't have back? The way she could dance and dive and ride a bike?

WENDY. Most people *like* to dwell on their golden years.

GREG. 'Most people'? Who are they? The ones you serve up in your talk-shows? Acting out their fashionable prahblems? Those 'people'?

MARK. Shall I turn this off?

WENDY. No. *I'm* enjoying it if she's not.

IMOGEN. Who's that young man with you all on Piazza San Marco?

WENDY. Oh, he was very good to me after your father left. (*Caresses and kisses* MARK.) Don't be jealous, darling.

IMOGEN. Grandpa's looking frail there.

GREG. He hadn't got long to go.

They all exclaim at the video, waking ALICE.

MARK. Well played, sir!

ALICE looks at the screen, suddenly stands and moves away. The rest go on watching and responding.

Music.

ALICE. He tried to bluster, poor old sod, shouting about cutting Wendy out of his will, but all he left was a few bills she had to settle. And now they want me in a single room in some fucking awful home with all those old dames dribbling into their cardigans!

She shouts into WENDY*'s ear.*

What'll happen then to my lovely walnut-veneer wardrobe? Out on a skip . . . gone for War on Want? Help The Aged? And the double bed I shared with his Nibs for half a life-time . . . him and – . . . well, not that many. One or two . . . which *you* knew all about, coming home early from school, pounding upstairs to tell me you'd won a merit star for Scripture and finding me there with What-was-his-name? But bless your heart, you didn't let on just now when he turned up acting the goat with your father at the cricket fixture. That was thoughtful. It wouldn't do for Imogen to think her Nana was fast. Oh, you *are* a good girl, really, still Mummy's good little girl, yes you are. Sometimes I'd like to scrunch you up. You mustn't mind what I say. Only don't let them put me in that place, there's a sweetheart. You can save me. It's Greg and Christine want me put away. My own little boy that used to take me for cocktails at the Mauretania. (*Shouting into his face.*) Before you met that first stuck-up article you married. No, *that* was Christine. Made you as toffee-nosed as she was. Too good for this earth so packed it in and left it early. This new one's Jill.

In her own time, she resumes her place. Then:

'Jill' reminds me: *his* name was Jack.

She sleeps as the lights fade to black.

End of Act One.

ACT TWO

As at end of last act. Five seconds pass.

MARK. She in the land of the living?

> *Lights up again, to about half.* ALICE*'s eyes shut.*

IMOGEN. It's hard to tell. I think she's asleep.

GREG. She's taken to eavesdropping with her eyes closed.

IMOGEN. Just resting them perhaps.

> *She smooths* ALICE*'s hair.*

WENDY (*standing*). That talk of a Jimmie has made me want
to go . . . Mark, try the studio again.

MARK. Shall I turn this off? She isn't watching.

GREG. Leave it. I'm enjoying it in a grisly way.

> *They move to the house door, leaving* GREG, IMOGEN *and*
> ALICE. *Lights go almost to nothing. Seconds pass.*
>
> *Light increases, the video flickering.* ALICE *dozing.*
>
> *Upstage of her we see* GREG *and* IMOGEN, *in a*
> *passionate embrace. No-one else present.* ALICE *stirs for a*
> *moment. They freeze.*

IMOGEN. Nana?

> *No answer. They kiss again.*

GREG. She called me 'Uncle'. Your Uncle Greg. Thank Christ
you never did.

IMOGEN. Perhaps if *I* had, this may never have happened.

GREG (*caressing her*). Think so? Like, when I came to lecture
at your college? If you'd called me 'uncle' before the Greek
meal and the Ouzo and bottle of red Dimestica . . . and
sharing a joint or two in your top-floor flat –

IMOGEN. Don't, Greg, please, that only / makes it worse –

GREG. – you think the table of consanguinity would have made us pull back? Like it did with all those family friends who got called 'aunt' and 'uncle' when I was a boy?

IMOGEN. Perhaps that was the purpose? To stifle the thought of incest before it could draw breath?

GREG. Incest? With them? Those aunts with strings of cultured pearls and knitting and Amami-waves . . .

IMOGEN. Was it to give them a status in the tribe then? Does *any*one use those titles now?

GREG. Only people as old as Mum.

IMOGEN. Pretty soon even 'Mum' and 'Dad' may be ageist. She already won't have 'grandma'. No roles left for the old to play. Not even Mister and Missis. No authority.

He caresses her again. She evades him.

No, no, no . . . it's wrong. I love Jill and respect her. Otherwise everything would be a breeze.

GREG. What should we do? Take off? Let's then. Just go. Today. Come on. What's stopping us?

IMOGEN. We agreed we'd never hurt her.

GREG. We shan't. She's got all those custody cases. I come second.

IMOGEN. Bad enough it's happened. Now it must stay between *us* . . . You promised me if I'd go on seeing you, / you wouldn't ever –

GREG. You've made me twenty years younger. I was dying on my feet. One of the walking wounded.

IMOGEN. That wasn't her fault.

GREG. No. Nor mine. Just life's. Without you, I'd die again.

IMOGEN. So why risk losing me?

GREG. I'm afraid you'll meet someone else, your own age. Honest, it would be the death of me. But Jill could cope. She's tougher than me.

They hear someone coming and move apart. MARK enters and moves towards the TV. ALICE shuts her eyes.

MARK. She still not watching?

IMOGEN. Fast asleep.

GREG. It's not very flattering to you in the trade but for most of us television's to sleep to.

MARK. That's right. The bright light's hypnotic.

He switches off the video. Lights to full.

ALICE. What a relief. That blessed video was going through my head. D'you think that's how I want to spend my only day with the family? Do that any time. Like in those Homes.

GREG. How d'you know? You wouldn't even go and see.

WENDY and JILL come in from upstairs.

ALICE. The instant they're woken up they want that screen on to calm their nerves. And till it does, the Chinkey girls make their beds jabbering and giggling while the poor old buggers stare at the light, waiting for a word they can understand.

IMOGEN. Chinese are great carers. Their Confucian philosophy is based on ancestor worship.

ALICE. You mean they don't put their parents in prison just for getting old? I see, as the blind man said –

GREG. Prison?! It's going to cost us all a fortune.

MARK. Prisons do.

He returns the videotape to its box.

GREG. Hullo, love. Done your report?

JILL. I heard Wendy come from the bathroom and caught her and convinced her I must come down / and talk it over.

WENDY. We've already made a start.

IMOGEN. Oh but Nana's right. This is her day. We should do what *she* wants.

ALICE *takes her hand, squeezes and kisses it*.

GREG. Like what? Eh, Mum? What *do* you want?

ALICE. A good time. Everybody happy. Not some old film or rabbiting on about people I've never heard of.

She dabs at her eyes with a tissue and throws it in the bin.

GREG. She usually keeps this till after *you*'ve all gone. 'Your blessed sister rabbiting on about life in London and all the famous people she knows and we only ever see on the screen. I sat there like a blessed fish, mouth opening and shutting, / never getting a word out.'

ALICE. I ask you, that / sound like me?

GREG. Well, now you've got the floor. We're all ears.

ALICE. What?

IMOGEN. *Anyone* would be struck dumb.

GREG. This is the matriarch's chance to hand down some irreducible nugget of wisdom. The elder of the tribe with her young sitting about her in the firelit circle. Nothing to say? Oh dear.

He again waits for ALICE *to speak*.

ALICE. You're looking tired, Gregory. D'you think your uncle looks tired, Imogen? They used to say that's a sign of an uneasy conscience.

JILL. God knows what about then.

GREG. I know! Our family tree! I love that one. And lo, Uncle Sidney took a wife and her name was Winnie and she bare him Bert and Margery and Edie –

ALICE. He likes to make fun of his mother.

WENDY. And Bert did take to wife Dorothy and twins leapt in her womb and she did bear him Fred and Percy –

ALICE (*delighted*). I never listen!

WENDY. And lo, they could find no labour and went to dwell in a far-off land calling itself Vancouver.

ALICE. No, that wasn't Dorothy's boys. That was Tilda's boys.

GREG. And Fred took to wife Marylou and she bare him Sigourney –

WENDY. And Tiffany.

ALICE. No, Marylou married Jack and came back during the war as a soldier . . . but you wouldn't remember him, son.

GREG. I'd only just been begat.

WENDY. I remember him.

ALICE looks at her then away.

GREG. She's got us doing it again.

ALICE. Who's 'she'?

MARK. The cat's mother.

IMOGEN. We started giving our presents but got waylaid. So here's mine.

She gives her a wrapped package, which ALICE *starts opening.*

ALICE. Well, I thought I wasn't to get anything but some blessed film from before the Ark.

IMOGEN. Something for your flat.

JILL. Then I hope it's portable.

ALICE. What is it? A picture? Yes, a picture in a frame! . . . No, just a frame. Oh dear . . . You forgot the picture, love. Never mind.

IMOGEN. So you can frame whichever photo you like.

WENDY. It's simply beautiful. Genuine Art Nouveau, from about the time you were born, d'you see?

IMOGEN. I found it in a little village shop. The woman had no idea how much to charge. She asked ten pounds but in the end I made her take more.

WENDY. Five times more.

IMOGEN. Mother!

ALICE (*bitterly*). An antique, like me. Well, it's the thought that counts. Give Nana a hug.

GREG. Here's mine. I didn't bother to wrap it because last time you complained it was hard to open.

GREG *starts a CD of Paul Robeson.* IMOGEN *is upset by* ALICE'*s response.*

ALICE (*joining in*).
Oh, ma babbie, ma curly-headed babbie,
Yoh pappy's in de cotton-field
A-dum-de-dum-de-dah . . .

My lord, that's from before the Ark. Paul Robeson used to sing it.

GREG. This *is* Paul Robeson.

ALICE. No, he had a much deeper voice.

She hums along with the tune.

GREG. Maybe we remember everything as deeper than it was.

ALICE. Used to be one of my most-requested encores. At the firm's annual dinners.

She sings along, eyes closed. JILL *gives her a wrapped package.*

JILL. Many happy returns!

ALICE (*tearing off the wrapping*). Not another record of some sort?

JILL. Something to use when your friends come round . . . or with the ones you'll meet in your new home.

ALICE. What d'you say? New what?

MARK. New friends.

ALICE. Oh. Jigsaw, is it? I can't do jigsaws.

JILL. No, a game.

ALICE. Oh dear. I'm useless at games. But thanks anyway – and give Nana a nice big hug.

JILL *submits and moves off.* MARK *pours more wine for her;* IMOGEN *recovers and opens the game.*

IMOGEN. *Scruples.* Great!

ALICE. A frame without a picture, a record from before the Ark and some blessed game I shan't follow. What have I done to deserve this, eh, Philip?

MARK *joins the others as they talk.*

GREG. *You* never gave *us* anything but tokens. Book tokens, Boots tokens, / record tokens . . .

ALICE. I never know what you want.

WENDY. You never bothered. When we were young, Dad chose the presents.

ALICE. He loved all that showing-off in the shops. The great I-am.

IMOGEN. Nana! Your cards.

ALICE. Oh dear . . .

IMOGEN *holds out five playing cards to her and deals hands to the others.*

What have I got to do with them?

IMOGEN. Nothing for now. Just listen.

WENDY. Who starts? Jill? You know the game best.

JILL *looks at her cards, then around the family. She puts an Answer card face down.*

JILL. Imogen – here's your ethical dilemma, okay? You're in a car-park looking for a space. The only free one is reserved for the handicapped. Do you take it?

IMOGEN. Of course not.

JILL. Even though this is a *hospital* car-park and you're about to give birth and the contractions are coming fast and the baby may be brain-damaged / if it isn't born within –

IMOGEN. Is that on the card?

JILL. Doesn't have to be. You can improvise. That's the best part. Using what you know about the other players' characters to get the response that's on *this* card – yes, no or depends.

IMOGEN. Even then I don't think I'd use a handicapped person's space. Suppose *they* were in trouble?

MARK. Already are, aren't they, being handicapped?

JILL. Alright. Suppose another driver's about to take that space and your contractions are unbearable and he's obviously not disabled at all, but using an illegal sticker. *Now* would you push in?

IMOGEN (*shakes her head*). His being wrong wouldn't make it right.

JILL (*showing her card*). A pretty decisive 'no', I think. Q.E.D.

WENDY. Daughter, promise me when you get pregnant, you'll let *me* drive you to the hospital.

JILL. With Imogen, it's almost cheating. She'll *always* do the decent thing.

WENDY. But is that decent? Possibly birth-damaging a child for some / abstract moral principle –

JILL. Okay. How about this for you, Wendy?

MARK. You've already had a turn. / If it's Wendy's –

JILL (*reading from a card*). Your aged mother can no longer cope. Left alone, she could harm herself and others. Your relatives bear the brunt of looking after her and think the time / has come to get her taken into care . . .

WENDY. No, come on, Jill –

JILL. I thought you agreed. Now or never.

Lights have faded as ALICE *dozes. Then on again as* WENDY *shakes her.*

WENDY. Mum – your turn.

ALICE. What? Oh dear. Already? What do I have to do?

WENDY. Look at your answer card –

ALICE. It just says / 'depends'.

WENDY. No, don't – read it out. Okay, take another. Look at it. Now. Choose one of us who's most likely to give the answer on this card and read out the question.

ALICE. How am I supposed to know?

JILL. Wendy's your daughter, Greg's your son, I'm your daughter-in-law. You must have formed *some* notion of our characters.

ALICE. 'You learn that your teenage daughter is having an affair with an older married man. Do you warn her?'

MARK. Who?

ALICE. What?

MARK. Warn who? The daughter or the wife?

ALICE. Well, Wendy's hardly a teenager. And Greg's daughters are in Melbourne and Africa.

WENDY. For Chrissake, Mum, it's not about *us*. It's a hypothetical moral dilemma.

ALICE. That case I'd hold my tongue. They'd none of them thank me. / No good ever comes –

JILL. *You're* not supposed to answer.

ALICE. I knew I'd do something wrong. You play without me. I'll sit and watch.

JILL. No good ever comes from what?

ALICE. Interfering. Causes bad feeling. Like when that fellow on the radio called Wendy an interfering busybody.

WENDY. What? Which fellow / was that?

ALICE. And in *The Sun*, when they said you were past your sell-by date. I wanted to call out 'don't you dare, that's my little girl you're talking about, not some packet of spare ribs'.

MARK. Little girl?

ALICE. And Gregory, he'll always be my little boy . . . in his knitted rompers and later on his school cap pulled down over one eye, bless him.

JILL. Oh, not the famous architect? Not Gregory Usher, F.R.I.B.A.? The man who changed the skyline of his native city? Just the rompers / and the cap?

ALICE. Don't mention his letters to me, Christine, when we all know he could have had a C.B.E.

JILL. Commander of a British Empire that hasn't existed for fifty years? That what you wanted your son to be?

GREG. Let it go, love.

ALICE. Oh, that wicked speech when you said why you'd turned it down. I couldn't show my face for a week at the off-licence I was so ashamed. Got dog muck sent him through the Royal Mail. Not only insulted the Queen but all the city bigwigs by asking how long were they going to leave Bristol in ruins as though the blitz was yesterday . . . and even after that, they still let you go on putting up those eyesores.

IMOGEN. Eyesores? Nana, / how could you?

ALICE. So you can hardly complain now they're going to pull them down.

GREG. Yes, next Sunday. A great day out. Local media. Down they go. Then play it backwards and up they go again. Which just about sums up the Brutish Isles at the moment. Laugh at everything. Nothing matters.

ALICE. Made too many enemies, son. Bit the hands that fed you. But Don't-Care was *made* to care.

GREG. Ah! The whole Modernist movement in a nutshell: Don't-care was made to care.

JILL. Go on, someone – slums of the future.

IMOGEN. I'd always thought that till Greg came to talk to my students and showed they were actually utopias. Towers, he

said, where the poor could turn their faces to the sun.
People who'd spent their lives in pits digging coal would be
in the sky among pools and roof gardens.

GREG (*with a sad shake of the head*). Esprit de Cor-busier.
Middlesborough twinned with Marseilles. We were so
cocky we believed we could change the weather!

IMOGEN. It was a beautiful dream that reckoned without the
mean-spirited / and stupid . . .

GREG. It was doomed. Don't-care was made to care. Even in
Marseilles the first tenants filled Corb's new world with
canary-cages and plaster ducks. My first tower's a no-go
area.

JILL. I could never take to Corbusier. Machines for Living?
Has anyone got the right to tell us how to live? Leave alone
a Frog?

Lights dim on ALICE *as she dozes*.

GREG. He was Swiss actually.

JILL. Even worse.

GREG. He reminded us that once, long ago, the cathedrals
were white.

IMOGEN. Oh Jill, what a vision! An end to the sort of
structures that kept people apart.

JILL. What if they *wanted* to be apart?

IMOGEN. They didn't know what they wanted.

JILL. But you do?

IMOGEN. They'd been made vicious like trained guard-dogs.
They had to learn to live better.

JILL. Don't-care was made to care?

GREG. In that talk you heard I was a lapsed Christian talking
about a God that failed. I thought the ill-nature we saw
everywhere was due to the way they'd been treated. Change
the regime and brutes will be angels. A delusion that's led
to our streets being like Calcutta's. We thought the mad and

vicious could be trusted and handed the asylum to the
lunatics. If we don't learn to submit our greed to the larger
good there won't be any good left. Or much of anything / in
fact –

MARK. All politics is you-scratch-my-back.

GREG. No, we're saying, Mark, that the architectural and
social issues were far more complex / than whether I talked
back to some local suits –

MARK. It's always Them and Us. Basically.

GREG. Well, not quite. I'd be*come* one / of Them –

MARK. At the end of the day any of us steps out of line we
get screwed. On a daily basis.

WENDY. No more, love. Highly complex argument. O.o.d.

JILL. Can we talk about Alice?

Light up on ALICE *as she stirs.*

IMOGEN. O.o.d?

MARK. Out of depth. Meaning me.

ALICE. Don't let her get away with that, young man. She'll
have you for breakfast if you let her. She may control the
purse-strings but that doesn't mean you can't stand / up to
her.

WENDY. Button it, Mum. Zip it up. Okay?

MARK. No, love, I know basically what I'm talking about
here: Masons, Mormons, army officers, royals, councillors,
policemen, customs and excise / bastards –

WENDY. Yes, dear, okay . . .

MARK. – rich bitches who don't even remember your name
after six weeks – and I don't mean you, love . . .

WENDY. Who then exactly, / if *not* me?

MARK. It's always Them and Us . . . the whole of society
needs overturning. Start again, only this time with us guys
calling the shots, right?

GREG. Right, yes. That was *my* ideal as well. We the people up there, / with panoramic views of –

MARK. No, not me. Not *my* lot.

GREG. It was in fact *all* about 'your lot' / and your lot spat on their chance –

MARK. What I mean, for 'us' there weren't that many options, right? Shovelling shit, playing football or going for a soldier. I did my share of shit-shovelling. For a year after school I was a slaughterman, prodding cows on with electric prongs, killing them with stun-guns. (*And as one or two make disgusted sounds.*) Oh, that's the kind part, the killing. So my mate and me signed on.

IMOGEN. For the army? Poor Mark.

MARK. Reckoned we'd only be changing one sort of gun for another. We thought: sooner be paras. Only now *we* were the ones being prodded on, right? into the shambles. All round the Falls Road, watching soft-core videos in the barracks and patrolling the streets of a lot of other poor bastards who never had no other chance but being talked down to by English toffs with plummy voices. But we were the targets they could *see* so it was my mate got shot, not some snotnose in Stormont. After that I done a runner.

WENDY. Did.

IMOGEN. Mother!

WENDY. He wants me to, don't you?

MARK. Yeah.

GREG. Deserted?

MARK. For two years, then had to serve out my sentence and the rest of my tour. Joined the Spandau Ballet.

IMOGEN. Really? Weren't they very big in the eighties?

MARK. Not the band. They only took their name from the drill we did at Spandau. Guarding Hess.

GREG. Rudolf Hess?

JILL. Hitler's second-in-command? What was he like?

MARK. Few pfenigs short of a mark. Liked tickling trout in the prison pool. And inspecting the guard. Reporting us if we got the drill wrong.

GREG. An old Nazi inspecting soldiers of the winning side?

MARK. That was how we saw ourselves, yeah. Flash, right? Cool. Conquering heroes. Wrong, right? Shit-shovellers in uniform. So I was shot at, wounded, left for dead in a Belfast gutter. Went AWOL, got buggered in the brig, sent back to be shot at again. Done drugs. Had more bad trips than Thomas Cook. Well, now I'm out of it, thanks to Wendy. In the lifeboat. From security guard to media executive in one jump, basically. Can't be bad, right?

He kisses her again. They all watch as she returns his embrace. Then MARK *looks at his watch.*

Listen, love, how'd it be if I break ranks for a bit? Is there an offie nearby, Greg? Only we're out of vodka.

WENDY. Make do with beer.

GREG. We don't drink it, sorry.

MARK. And cigarettes.

WENDY. Fifteen minutes max.

MARK. Tops.

WENDY. Take the mobile.

MARK. Still can't risk it, can you? Even in the Mallet they made me a trustie. Let me out shopping with the screws.

WENDY. I only mean in case we have to change our plans.

MARK. Not a lapdog on a lead, see?

WENDY. It's the opposite. I'm nervous when I'm off yours. But you know that, love.

She kisses him.

MARK. Yeah. So to make town by half past eight, we need the six-fifteen from Parkway.

JILL. You're leaving in three hours?

ALICE. I thought you said you were staying over.

WENDY. Never. I'm due at an awards dinner / at Grosvenor House –

ALICE. Haven't you got enough blessed awards?

WENDY. Not *getting* tonight. Presenting. Agreed to it yonks ago. I wasn't to know you'd fall.

JILL. You knew it was her birthday.

MARK. You can see it tomorrow, by the way, on Three.

ALICE. I don't want to watch my little girl on a screen. I want her here, to have and hold . . .

She gives WENDY *a bear-hug.*

Is that too much to ask? On Mummy's birthday?

WENDY. Which one?

ALICE. What?

WENDY. Which birthday is it? Come on, Mum. Say it or I'm leaving right now. (*Moving towards the door.*) Not twenty-one but – ?

ALICE. Oh dear. Eighty-five.

Everyone cheers and applauds, MARK *and* IMOGEN *whooping.*

WENDY. There. That wasn't too bad, was it? A first faltering step towards reality.

ALICE. Doesn't seem fair that the worst of life is at the end. The bit you remember when you pass on.

IMOGEN (*kissing her*). Nana, you've got many wonderful years to come.

ALICE. As long as we know.

MARK. See you then. Cheers.

He goes. Front door slammed off. Lights flicker briefly but remain low. ALICE *in her own world.*

WENDY. It frightens me how much he needs me. If I'm to build his confidence, I must show I trust him.

JILL. So can't you? Why should he run away from all you give him?

WENDY. Oh, you think he loves me only for what I give him? Older woman and kept boy? Well, you've got your battered wives and kids. And Mark's my lame dog. Belfast's only his alibi. He was wounded long before, by dear old Family Life. Abused by Uncle, bullied by Dad, a drunk by twenty, a druggie by twenty-five –

GREG. He's lived more in thirty years than I have in fifty-five. Beside him – Mum's right – I'm a babbie in rompers!

ALICE (*to herself*). Bless his heart!

JILL. Never mind Mark, he's *your* problem. Ours is the birthday girl. And how to guarantee her many happy returns.

IMOGEN (*low voice, aside*). Why don't you all go and talk it over upstairs?

GREG. What, without her?

IMOGEN. Certainly not in front of her. She may hear.

JILL. You think that's kinder? It's only too easy for you coming down on a day-return with your unblemished conscience, but we have to carry the can when she hurts herself.

ALICE (*unheard*). Anyone think I was a parcel.

JILL. And I mean *literally* carry it, up and down, when she comes to our country place and can't reach the ground-floor toilet. And have her belching and farting through the Sunday lunch she insists I cook her.

ALICE (*unheard*). What if I talked about you like that in company?

JILL. I gave her honey once by mistake instead of mustard, she spread it on her meat and never knew.

ALICE (*unheard*). D'you think I was going to *tell* you the mustard tasted off?

WENDY. I know, my loves.

ALICE (*unheard*). I wish I had now. That's the thanks you get / for trying to be kind –

WENDY. If only there was some other way.

IMOGEN. There is.

JILL. What?

GREG. Her own suggestion: leave her lying on the bathroom floor.

IMOGEN. No, Greg. She might hear you.

JILL. She's asleep.

GREG. Then get back in the car and drive home? Allow a few hours to pass? Watch a video. Go back to make sure it's over? But it would only take one interfering home-help carrying tales –

IMOGEN. I know you're only joking but – . . .

JILL. Alright, Imogen, what's this other way?

IMOGEN. That she should live with each of us in turn.

JILL. A rota system?

IMOGEN. Turn and turn-about, yes.

WENDY. Now hold it right there!

IMOGEN. A few months with me, in Mum's penthouse another few, back here with you, / then me again . . .

WENDY. Love, I live on the seventh floor.

IMOGEN. You've got a lift.

WENDY. She'd never learn how to *work* the lift. She'd be found impaled by the door, gone walkabout, lost in the boiler-room. Women in her day never worked *any*thing. Just sat looking pretty.

GREG. Which she certainly was.

They all look at her, dozing.

WENDY. Men drove the cars. She couldn't even use a phone till I taught her. Listening to the mouthpiece – 'allo . . . allo?' . . .

GREG. So pretty once.

JILL. I grew up in a loving family. Being caught up in one like this is better than a course in domestic violence.

IMOGEN. Why don't you both love her? What did she do?

WENDY. I've spent a fortune on shrinks trying to answer that.

Lights brighten slightly as ALICE *stirs and murmurs.*

JILL. What's she mumbling on about now?

IMOGEN. Was she very fond of Grandpa?

WENDY. In those days couples stayed together, bound by mutual loathing. They couldn't teach *us* how to love because they neither of them knew.

IMOGEN. You think it must be taught?

WENDY. By osmosis. Don't scoff, daughter dear, I did set you / an example –

IMOGEN. / I wasn't scoffing –

WENDY. Loved not wisely but too well. Who said that? But poor Nana married for advancement. Security. When she was young, finding a man with a house up the hill and a car and a cheque-book meant a lot more than love.

JILL. I hope she's got her rubbers on.

IMOGEN. Oh, Jill!

JILL (*savagely*). That's why this is urgent! Residential homes won't take incontinents. Miss that deadline, you're talking hospitals.

GREG. Giggling fillies with Walkmans turned up loud to shut out the patients' cries for help.

IMOGEN. Fillies? Really, Greg!

GREG. That's not chauvinism. Short for Filipinos. At least the Chinese woman in the home we've earmarked wished us a Happy Christmas.

JILL. Such a good try we didn't like to point out it was December thirty-first.

IMOGEN. New Year's more important to them.

Telephone rings off. Lights flicker and go to half, favouring ALICE. GREG goes off to answer. The others, in penumbra, may chat silently, clear up, come and go.

ALICE. They don't have to tell me. I went for tea with this old dear I met in the shopping mall. I wouldn't go when Greg and Whatsername asked me to, case they saw it as a white flag. Well, talk about stranded whales. And a few even looking down their noses, putting on the Clifton Spa, as much as to say 'tuppence to talk to us'. Comical really. I wanted to say 'Did *you* have a car in 1930?'. I did remark to my friend 'It's a mystery they can afford the fees.' And she said 'All sorts can afford Clifton these days.' I said 'So I see'. She said 'Oh, they're not so bad when you get to know them.' I said 'I shan't be here long enough.' And while we were in the cupboard she called a bedroom, I heard a window-cleaner tell his mate: 'I'd die of shame before I put my mother in one of these.' Only a common labouring man but he didn't need lessons in loving his mother. And blow me, if she didn't start crying like a babbie. I said 'You've only yourself to blame. You should have kicked and screamed before you let them . . . '

GREG has returned, with a cordless phone.

GREG. Mum. Wake up.

Lights to full.

ALICE. I'm not asleep.

GREG. Your granddaughter. You remember Barbara? And Alice begat Greg and he also took him a wife and she bare him two sons and a daughter? And when they were full-

grown they went to dwell in far-off lands and begat
Benedict and Caroline –

ALICE (*looking about*). Young Barbara? Come all this way to
be with her Nana? Come and give Nana a nice big hug.

IMOGEN. No, Nana, on the phone.

ALICE. What's she want then? I hope it's not about gravy
again.

GREG (*explaining*). Barbara rang the other day when her
mother was at work to ask Mum how to make gravy.

ALICE. I mean, couldn't she have asked a neighbour? Doesn't
anyone know how to make gravy in Melbourne?'

IMOGEN. No, to wish you happy returns.

ALICE. From all across the world? Oh dear . . .

GREG (*to phone*). No, love, they haven't come yet. Unless we
missed the bell. Here's Mum. Ask after the children.

ALICE. Oh, Benny and Carrie . . . bless their hearts, yes. (*Very
loud into the phone.*) Hullo? Barbee?

GREG. No need to shout. You're being bounced off a satellite.
And it's Barbara, not Barbee. She's not a doll who asks to
go to the comfort station when you pull a string in her
navel.

WENDY. Another way of freezing us all in childhood.

ALICE *listens, as much to the family as the phone.*

GREG. I was shocked myself about the gravy. I remember the
first Moon broadcast. The fabulous future! One giant step
for mankind. Now used for a recipe for gravy.

IMOGEN. If it makes her happy –

GREG. We grew up in a more frugal time.

WENDY. Frugal? You make it sound desirable. There was
nothing of anything!

ALICE. Yes, well Nana can't seem to hear you all that well. So
bye-bye, Barbee, and god bless.

Turns off and gives him back the phone.

GREG. Hello? . . . gone. How d'you know I didn't want to talk to my daughter again?

ALICE. You couldn't hear, from all that way off.

GREG. *I* heard, as though she was next-door.

WENDY. I'd have liked a word too. What did she say?

ALICE. Only to know how to make gravy.

JILL. That was last week.

ALICE. I can smell something burning *now*. Don't tell me I've left the blessed roast on?

JILL. Oh, fuck! The snacks in the oven.

She hurries off through a cloud of smoke to the kitchen.

GREG. Don't worry, love, it's not your fault. We all forgot.

IMOGEN. Poor Jill!

They both follow JILL *off.*

ALICE. She's a good enough girl but I can't see why Greg's quite so blessed smitten with her, can you? Poor lamb. Forever sending out for Tandoori. She can only manage the Michaelwave.

WENDY*'s mobile rings.*

WENDY. Yeah? Who? . . . Melissa? Put on Joanna . . . what meeting, on a Sunday? And why is her mobile off? . . . Well, she'd better turn it on a.s.a.p. or I'll want to know what the – / . . . she said what?

ALICE. You seen their bedroom? Talk about the teddy-bears' picnic. Poor Gregory'd have loved more babbies.

WENDY. . . . Look, just tell her I'm on the case. (*Glancing at* ALICE *in passing.*) Yeah, researching . . . uh? . . . we've *done* the menopause . . . and mastectomy, twice, . . . what? One each side? Ho, ho, funny! And M.E., yes, and H.R.T. and P.M.T. and I.V.F. . . . abortion we've done to death, yes, but not Ageing, not in depth. It's worth an entire series.

For some moments she stands looking at ALICE.

Anyway why am I talking to the monkey? Where's the organ-grinder? . . . so tell her to ring me back and quick.

Turns off.

Fucking cow! Where did I leave that taxi number?

She goes off to the front hall.

Lights to black as ALICE *sleeps. Music.*

After some seconds, lights to a quarter.

IMOGEN *moves across from the kitchen door, looks off to see* WENDY, *shuts door firmly. Checks* ALICE's *eyes are closed.* GREG *follows. He and* IMOGEN *meet upstage, out of* ALICE's *sight, embrace and kiss, speak in undertones.*

IMOGEN. No . . . not here . . . Mum's in the hall.

GREG. And Jill's in the kitchen.

IMOGEN. Yes, and I love and respect her too much ever to hurt her.

He goes on making love to her.

GREG. Oh, she's strong, don't you know that? Too strong for me. Let's go before she squeezes me to death. Please –

IMOGEN (*breaking away*). We must stop this now.

GREG. Let me follow you tomorrow. I'll tell Jill tonight after you've all gone.

IMOGEN. You only ask because you know I won't say yes.

GREG. Oh, try me –

Door opens and WENDY *comes back, talking into phone.*

WENDY. . . . soon as you like. I'm ready now . . . Bristol Parkway, yeah . . . right. (*Turns off.*)

GREG (*collecting glasses, going off*). Better help Jill.

WENDY. Sweetheart, we must catch the next train. That cow Joanna's trying to axe the series. In a meeting? To *me*?!

IMOGEN. Leave Nana's birthday / halfway through?

WENDY. I can't afford not to. Where would she be if I had no
job? Love, you know the game. It's (*Makes quote marks.*)
'who leaves Rome loses Rome', believe me. A coup d'état.
Caesar going to Egypt, Alexander to wherever-it-was, /
Thatcher to Paris, –

IMOGEN. So – what can you *do*?

WENDY. Fight. I thought I'd be safe on my mother's birthday.
And a Sunday?

IMOGEN. Where's Mark? Won't you need him?

WENDY. Fallen among friends, I dare say.

IMOGEN. You're walking out on him too?

WENDY. If he's not here / when I need him most –

IMOGEN. Why don't you let go? You've already had one
coronary.

WENDY. No choice. I should have told you all sooner: the
revenue have closed a loophole, so after next month Mum's
rent can't be paid to the company, and I'll need to earn even
more to cover tax.

ALICE *groans. They look at her.*

Is she with us?

IMOGEN. Shall I wake her up?

WENDY. No. Be ready to leave. I've called a cab.

IMOGEN. I'm not going. You don't need me. But Jill does.
Greg and Jill need to know one of us / cares enough –

ALICE (*sings*).
'Wish me luck as you wave me goodbye . . .
Ta-da-dee, ta-da-dee um-dee-dum . . . '

IMOGEN *and* WENDY *watch her.*

That's the lot . . . move along inside . . . hold tight! Go
ahead, driver . . .

WENDY. She's a clippie again. Her finest hour.

ALICE. . . . . any more fares?

IMOGEN. She rang off last Sunday saying her bus would be leaving without her.

WENDY. D'you ring her *every* Sunday?

IMOGEN. Sometimes in the week instead.

WENDY (*embracing her*). My dear, why don't you think of someone else but yourself for once?

IMOGEN (*after a pause*). Oh, right, you're being ironic.

WENDY. There's a limit to how much we can help others. I wanted to talk on the train but you sat by Mark and somehow . . . tell me, are you happy in that awful Midlands polytechnic?

IMOGEN. University.

WENDY. With your First Class Honours, you could have been an Oxbridge don.

IMOGEN. Bottles of old port aren't how I see life today.

WENDY. But a Victorian orphanage is?

IMOGEN. Nobody's into that snobbery any more, Mother. We're too busy trying to save the planet.

WENDY. Save yourself. Come and live in town. Join my team. Learn the job. Inherit the slot.

IMOGEN *shakes her head. The front doorbell rings and* IMOGEN *goes to answer.* WENDY *crouches by* ALICE's *chair.*

Mum! Mother! I know you're awake, come on . . .

Lights up.

ALICE. I must have nodded off. Hardly any wonder when no-one talks to me. I could sit here all day and none of you would even know if I'd passed on.

WENDY. Look, I'm sorry but I just can't stay.

ALICE. You've only just arrived.

WENDY. It was terrific seeing you. We must talk about you coming up for a weekend, soon as I'm through this night of the long knives –

GREG and JILL *come from the kitchen with plates of snacks.*

GREG. Burnt to a crisp. In fact, we wonder if they'll *do* as crisps?

ALICE. Your sister's going back to blessed London.

JILL. What?

ALICE. What d'you think of her? She must love those buzz-bombs.

WENDY. Got to deal with the KGB. The Gang of Four.

JILL. Nothing's sorted! That's what this day was for!

WENDY. Jill, I'm sorry as hell. This is truly my anus horribilis but if they pull the plug on the new series, we'll all be down the tube –

JILL. We're there already.

WENDY. Hey, who pays the lion's share of her rent?

JILL. You do, to yourself. Wendy Usher Limited which owns the flat.

WENDY. It's a company asset. All in the family. You're all directors. And if Wendy Usher Live is dropped, there'll be nothing left of Wendy Usher Limited and not much of Wendy Usher either. (*Seeing* IMOGEN *return with flowers.*) Is it the minicab?

IMOGEN. No. Flowers. From different people but all delivered at once. There's more.

She leaves the elaborate bouquets and goes.

GREG. Look at these. All the way from Melbourne. And these from Indonesia.

ALICE. It's a miracle they keep so fresh.

GREG. Yes. And what lovely spring flowers grow in the kitchen gardens of Jakarta.

JILL. These are from us.

IMOGEN (*re-entering with more*). And more – from your social club and Auntie Doris in Spain.

They arrange the flowers around her. GREG *takes a flash-photo.*

ALICE. More a funeral than a birthday. I feel like I've been laid out.

The others see it's true. The effect is like a lying-in-state.

WENDY. Don't, Mum, please.

ALICE. Take a last look at mother before you rush off. Next time you see her, she may well be . . .

She sobs and reaches for IMOGEN *as she approaches.*

You won't leave Nana, will you, love?

IMOGEN. Of course not.

WENDY. Lord, what am I doing?

She and IMOGEN *kneel and crouch by* ALICE.

JILL. So if her flat's a family asset, why not sell it and use the interest to buy a place in the sunset?

IMOGEN. Don't talk like this in front of Nana –

JILL. Your mother's forcing us to.

Doorbell. GREG *looks through the front window.*

GREG. Minicab!

WENDY (*rising painfully from her knees*). Imo dear, stay till Mark comes. / Bring him on a later train.

IMOGEN. *If* he comes –

WENDY. He can't survive unscathed without me.

GREG. Hasn't he survived Belfast unscathed?

WENDY. No. That he hasn't.

JILL. So where does this leave *us*?

WENDY. Bear with me, Jill. Let's exchange e-mails. Or come
for a weekend, talk it through. Mum . . . Many happy
returns. (*Kisses* ALICE, *who turns her head away*.) Bye,
Greg, we'll sort this out, believe me.

JILL (*dodging the kiss*). Fuck you!

WENDY *goes*.

No idea, has she? How can I take a weekend off? With all
those desperate families waiting on my word, –

But GREG's *eyes are on* IMOGEN *as she kneels by* ALICE.

IMOGEN. Nana . . . I'm still here. What can I get you? More
Bristol Cream?

ALICE. Where's these snacks we've heard so much about? It
must be nearly tea-time and we haven't even had dinner . . .
have we?

JILL (*to* IMOGEN). Parental genes are supposed to be
reshuffled in the child but you're a whole new pack of
cards. How will you ever find a decent enough chap?

IMOGEN. That betrays your age. We're not all holding our
breath for a man.

GREG. It's not p.c.

JILL. Incorrect and unfashionable doesn't always mean untrue.

IMOGEN. Anyway they're mostly busy or taken. The decent
chaps *I* know are up a tree in some forest they're going to
cut down for a supermart / or tunnelling / beneath some –

ALICE. One more on top and that's it! Ting!

IMOGEN. Alright, Nana . . .

GREG *looks among his LPs and CDs*.

ALICE. I hate blessed London. Bristol would have been the
capital if it hadn't been for one thing.

IMOGEN. What's that?

ALICE. The mud. So many ships got stuck in it. Your Dad always said that, Gregory –

GREG. Always, yes . . .

ALICE. I'm sick to death of hearing about their blitzes. We may not have their doodle-bugs but our whole city's been ablaze. Poor mother's house was hit, a bomb caught the gas-mains, she ran through the streets for shelter while I was safe in bed, not knowing. But we heard the bombs raining down and I said 'My God, those German swine!' and Buddy said 'Never you mind, honey, when we reach France, / we'll give them bastards hell for this – '

JILL (*to* GREG). *What* did she say?

GREG. Who's Buddy? Cousin Buddy from Calgary?

ALICE. What? No. Clifford. I meant Clifford. Your father. No, who mentioned Buddy? Anyway whenever he stayed with us, he slept downstairs on the sofa.

Pause. She looks about.

He said 'I'll give them, fucking Germans – '

The lights fade as she dozes. They watch.

GREG. He came visiting some years later. A dim little guy with no hair and a childless wife who said our kids were cute. 'They got 'em over there,' she said, 'they come on teevee, they give'em a dollar.'

Looks at ALICE.

So were they in bed together in the air-raid? When I was two?

JILL. Long ago and far away. Unimportant.

IMOGEN. Not to her.

ALICE (*singing*).
Long ago and far away
I dreamed a dream one day –
And now this dream is here beside me –
Da-dee-dum-dee-dum-dee-da –

GREG. So many lives pack up long before our hearts.

JILL. So she's left to us again and I'll make the decisions.
Apply to the council to find her a home, / make her sign the
committal form . . .

GREG. I'll handle all that.

JILL. That'll be the day. I must finish my report.

She goes by the 'front'.

IMOGEN. Jill's completely stressed out.

GREG (*embracing* IMOGEN). She doesn't need me. There's
nothing to stop us. Save me. I'm suffocating.

IMOGEN. Alright.

GREG. What?

IMOGEN. How shall we do it? Will you come to me in
Birmingham? Or shall we go straight from here? You'll
have to explain to Jill. Arrange all the details, who'll get
what . . . (*And, as* GREG *gapes at her*.) It's got to be
thought about.

GREG. Has it? Yes . . . right –

Front door bell. ALICE *stirs and lights come on.*

ALICE. I hope that's not one of those blessed telegrams from
the War office.

IMOGEN. There there, Nana . . .

GREG *stands paralysed.*

ALICE. Or a gypsy-woman selling pegs or violets, giving the
breast to some dark-eyed babbie.

IMOGEN. Are you going to answer it then?

ALICE. Mind you cross her palm with silver or she'll spit in
your face.

Before GREG *can go, a sound of disputing voices and*
MARK *comes in, fast and furious, a bottle of wine in each*

hand, followed by JILL *and* WENDY. *He goes to the window and stares out, then mimes drawing curtains across the window.*

Philip, don't let the old gipsy put a curse on you.

IMOGEN. Why do that in daylight?

WENDY. What's happened?

MARK. Don't ask.

WENDY. I just did.

ALICE. Oh, yes, there's a good boy, I'm sick to death of telling Gregory about those neighbours staring in / soon as we turn the lights on. .

MARK. Screw the neighbours. I'm talking serious grief here.

ALICE. I don't know what they've got against net.

MARK. Here, sweetheart, nice white for you.

ALICE *grabs the bottle he thrusts on her.*

ALICE. Oh dear . . .

JILL. When I went out, Wendy was sitting on our front wall. No sign of the cab she was supposed to take and Mark coming up the road like a bat / from hell and –

IMOGEN. Was that what stopped you? You saw Mark?

WENDY. So, tell us what you've been up to.

MARK. Turned out The Lord Raglan was a shooting-gallery and these dealers served me a paper. When I opened it in the bog, I saw right off it was a six-and-four. I sounded off and one tried to chiv me so I bolted. Plus, I sussed the narco squad was staking the place out so / I did a runner –

IMOGEN. Oh, not again.

WENDY. You swore you were clean. You'd done with all that.

GREG. All what? What's he talking about?

IMOGEN. The police may have seen him deal some stuff in a pub.

GREG. What, dope, drugs? And followed you back here?

WENDY. Poor foolish boy.

MARK. I couldn't handle how you kept putting me down about the way I talk. Making me feel this small, know what I mean? Had to psych myself up. You wasn't about to walk out on me?

WENDY. I was, yes, on all of you. Then I sat on the wall and thought to myself what-the-hell.

MARK. Which is when I come along?

WENDY. Came –

She chokes it back.

MARK. You couldn't handle all them slags alone. You need me for muscle.

ALICE. She knows once she left him, he'd be off. Wouldn't you, son? Once he'd got his hands on her money.

From now on no-one hears her. They gather on one side, leaving her on the other.

MARK. I can handle anything but being in love with someone that don't love me.

WENDY. Oh, but I do.

He's sunk to his knees, his head against her, like a child's.

MARK. So why d'you let me go off the rails like that?

WENDY. And why d'you always *do* it? To dare me? That it?

MARK. Don't ask. Every time I go on a trip may be the last I see of you and that would finish me. Without you I'd . . .

He sobs against her thigh. She holds his head.

ALICE. Poor babbie. He reminds me so much of Arnold that was after me before the war.

WENDY. Any sign of men outside?

GREG (*looking between the curtains*). None that I can see.

MARK. Not on the facing pavement neither?

WENDY. They weren't after you, love, only the dealers.

GREG. Have you brought any 'stuff' into the house?

MARK. I ditched it down a drain once I sussed they were the fuzz.

WENDY (*to the others*). He suffers from a heated imagination. (*To him.*) Watch my lips, Mark. There aren't any police.

ALICE. Police, on my birthday? Oh, no!

GREG. No worries then.

ALICE. That'd be just my luck.

WENDY. No worries anyway. If they come, I'll pull rank.

JILL. What rank is that?

GREG. The highest of all. Teevee celebrity.

ALICE. They came to our place only last week as we were sitting down to Christmas dinner, making out your father had been black-marketeering.

WENDY. I earned brownie-points last year with the boys in blue by giving airtime on my show to that constable's widow.

ALICE. That neighbour in the Salvation Army reckoned she saw him unload bacon from the car. Good job Dad was in the Masons. The police were very good about it.

WENDY. I just sat there and thought: what am I running to?

ALICE. Gregory, son, if they come to the door, mind you give the secret handshake.

WENDY. To another long-drawn-out battle to take a fortress I no longer want? To be allowed to pass the time of a lot of people / I'll never meet . . .

ALICE. There she goes again. / Talk talk talk talk . . .

WENDY. . . . and who know me only as so many flickering lines on a screen?

JILL. You'll excuse me not believing in yet another change of heart?

GREG (*at the window*). I've never thought of Arlington Villas as the Road to Damascus.

WENDY. It's been coming for some time. What makes Wendy run? What matters most? The Problems of Ageing or my actually aged Mum?

A single spot returns on ALICE.

ALICE. Her face that day when she came home and found me with – oh Lord, what's his name again?

The others and their dialogue now begin to fade and ALICE*'s light becomes stronger. We hear only fragments of their talk, mingling with sounds from the past: wartime songs, the bell and motor of a bus, bar-room laughter,* ALICE *herself singing 'Oh ma babbie', a bomb falling . . .*

Everyone called him Buddy. But his real name was Wilbur.

Where've you all gone? Don't keep moving where I can't hear you. Oh, that blessed monkey. Get him away from the window. Pull the net curtains across. Stop him showing off. Playing with hisself. Mucky little devil. I thought I'd left him behind in my wardrobe. Never reckoned he'd follow me here to the Avon Gorge hotel . . . I don't know where to put myself . . . See The Bridge beyond him, beyond that window? . . . My grandfather carried his trade across that bridge the day it opened in – when was it?

Trying to remember, she shakes her head. Lights go to black.

Pause. The others give a sudden laugh, waking ALICE, *and the lights brighten.*

He'll fall . . . that blessed monkey . . . stop him!

Lights flicker on and off, hovering on her for a few seconds. ALICE *slightly shakes her head.*

Now look . . . He's floating . . . flying out to sea. Oh dear . . .

The glass falls from her hand and all sounds suddenly cease, except for one note of music that hangs on for some moments, then itself gives out.

As does the last light.

The End.

A Nick Hern Book

So Long Life first published as a paperback original in 2000
by Nick Hern Books Limited, 14 Larden Road, London W3 7ST

So Long Life copyright © Peter Nichols 2000

Peter Nichols has asserted his right to be identified as
the author of this work

Typeset by Country Setting, Kingsdown, Kent CT14 8ES
Printed by Biddles, Guildford

Cover photo by Tony Ray-Jones, courtesy National Museum of
Photography, Film & Television/Science & Society Picture Library

A CIP catalogue record for this book is available from
the British Library

ISBN 1-85459-606-3